Daniel Boone

James Daugherty

DANIEL BOONE

by

James Daugherty

with

Original Lithographs in Color
by the Author

NEW YORK · THE VIKING PRESS
1939

INDIANA STATE
T.C. LIBRARY

To the Two Charles'

To my dad in remembrance of
our gorgeous adventures among books
and to my son in appreciation of
our rich companionship among pictures

TEACHING
MATERIALS
B
Boon

FIRST PUBLISHED OCTOBER 1939

COPYRIGHT 1939 BY JAMES DAUGHERTY

PUBLISHED BY THE VIKING PRESS

PRINTED IN THE UNITED STATES OF AMERICA BY W. C. D. GLASER

DISTRIBUTED IN CANADA BY THE MACMILLAN COMPANY OF CANADA, LTD.

INDIANA STATE
T.C. LIBRARY

Dear Colonel Boone:

Because I have just come back from Boonesborough, and the beauty and majesty of the Cumberlands, the Smokies, and the Tennessee Mountains are still aflame in stirring vistas of memory, and your image and fame are a great name echoing down the beautiful valleys, I am writing you a letter to tell you how it all seems a hundred years after, and of the thoughts that still linger and drift as one rides so swiftly and smoothly over the trails you trod so desperately.

I have driven down the Shenandoah, the great valley of Virginia, where the ghosts of gray Confederate lines still hold and break in the valley mists, and Marse Robert and Stonewall Jackson and Jeb Stuart are riding by.

Further on, in Tennessee, we found the sunny shallows of the Watauga dappled in the shade of large sycamores where the Cherokee chiefs traded Kentucky for a red shirt so long ago.

We found the little water-fall at Boone's Creek under which you hid from the pursuing warriors. We followed the wilderness trail (now a cement highway) along the beautiful winding Holston valley and across in the wild Clinch and Powell Mountains and their steep valleys to the long high gap in the Cumberlands, the famous gateway to Kentucky.

We climbed up to the dizzy "Pinnacle" and looked down far, east and west, on two worlds and four states. We followed the Cumberland among the steep somber shoulders of wild mountains near savage Harlan and out into rolling lovely Kentucky. It is still the wilderness road in places where the one-room log cabins stand high on the mountain sides, and lean and sullen barefoot folk stare gauntly at intruders from another world.

We were at the end of the Wilderness Road at last. It was a queer exciting feeling to be nearing Boonesborough, turning off the main highway at Turtle

[5]

236380

INDIANA STATE
T.C. LIBRARY

Creek, and sighting the long river-bend where the log fort had stood. I had a haunting sense that buckskin-clad men in fur caps would be hailing us at the next turn.

We swung off the road at an abandoned hotel and drove to the river. The old site of Boonesborough is a bathing resort, and, it being a Sunday in October, nobody was there. There is a dancing pavilion, and at the far end of a row of shabby summer cottages is the little stone inclosure that marks the site of the fort.

A few yards away from the river is a bronze tablet on a little stone monument telling about the Transylvania Company with Mr. Henderson's name in large letters. In smaller letters are listed the names of thirty men of the Wilderness Road band including yourself. Another tablet is "In pious and eternal memory of the First Christian Service in Kentucky on this hallowed spot."

A few yards away from the hallowed spot, a heap of tin cans, empty bottles, and refuse commemorates the passing of last summer's cottagers. But the beauty of the huge sycamores towering in the council hollow gives a majestic reverence that shames the gaudy language of the bronze inscriptions. We sat under them by the drowsing river which flows past the site of Boonesborough, with our thoughts of how your name had gone throughout the world to fire and kindle dreams. And here was the very spot where the thrilling climax to the drama was acted out, deserted on a Sunday afternoon and marked by the ardent bronze tablets and the rubbish heap and the shoddy empty cottages after a hundred years.

But the scene was true to the legend.

You never had any legal claim on Kentucky. You were not a leader of business enterprise like Mr. Henderson. You belonged to the Indian and the buffalo. You gave all and received nothing. You were a romantic. You neglected your opportunities to get in on the ground floor. You were a free singing rider in a lost dream.

But you kept your rendezvous with destiny. When history called for men of action you were there. And so your name still echoes in the mountain passes and

INDIANA STATE
T.C. LIBRARY

is a whisper and a heart-beat along the old trail. Your image is a living flame, ever young in the heart and bright dream of America marching on.

And so I have drawn the pictures and stumblingly written these words, because I believe you and your tough true breed are calling across a hundred years to young America:

"Rise up, you lanky sons of democracy,

    Of Tennessee, of Texas, Vermont, New Hampshire,

Mississippi, Ohio, Oregon, and the rest of the glorious brotherhood of States.

Remember Clark of Vincennes, Robertson of Watauga, Nolichucky Jack, Donaldson of the *Adventure*, Mansker and the Long Hunters, Mrs. Bean and the fighting pioneer women who made homes and bred Horse and Alligator sons in the snow drifts and hollow trees and log forts of the old frontier.

Pray to the God of your Fathers that their spirit be upon you.

That you may have the enduring courage to cut a clean straight path for a free people through the wilderness against oppression and aggression,

For generations marching on to higher freedoms

Riding toward the sun

Singing in the canebrakes

Singing in the tough spots

Chanting: Democracy, here we come.

Millions of cantankerous laughing sons and strong daughters

Shouting to the bullies, the tyrannies, the hosts of Darkness

Shouting with a seven-times-mighty shout of Jericho:

               NO SURRENDER."

And so, Daniel Boone, I wish you a hearty Tennessee Howdy and So Long.

James Daugherty

PIONEER BABIES

Kentucky cradles were never empty.
Torrents of fat naked babies overflowed from bulging cradles and
cluttered crowded cabins.
Wide solemn eyes peered from behind their mothers' skirts at strangers.
Tiny toddlers squealed gleefully to skin-clad daddies bringing home
fat turkeys from the forest.

Then they turned their toes toward the sundown.
They waddled West as soon as they could stagger.
They cooed and gurgled to the crimson sunset.
They reached their paws for a slice of the red pumpkin pie
going down over the purple hills.

They wrassled the wild cats and they romped with wolves.
They pulled the panthers by their tails.
They tackled tall turkey gobblers and ruined their pride.
They rolled in rapture down the Rappahannock.
They rafted in their cradles down the Ohio.
They climbed the Tuscaroras and they coasted down the Cumberlands

in three-cornered pants
and dug their toes into the black loam
of the fat bottom lands
to grow up tall and lean and towheaded
like the greenwaving tasseled Indian corn.

1730

I· OF A FRONTIER FAMILY

SQUIRE BOONE was a blacksmith of Berks County, Pennsylvania, who owned a prosperous farm near the frontier village of Reading. The pleasant ringing of hammer on iron made a peaceful music to the goodwife Sarah in the near-by snug log house, where she cooked and wove and washed and spun and managed the eleven husky children that made up the Boone family in the Seventeen Thirties.

From time to time she bundled off two or three of them to the small blab school a mile or so down the road where a crotchety schoolmaster with the aid of a well-worn hickory switch drummed into their tough skins the black arts of reading, 'riting, and 'rithmetic, or as much as they could hold. But they refused really to be hampered by the rules of spelling.

Otherwise they were quick learners and adept scholars in the arts and crafts by which men and women on the Allegheny frontier survived and prospered on the dark edge of the wilderness. Boys learned the easy way to swing an ax all day long, hold an ox-drawn plow on a straight furrow, mend a harness, and hitch a horse, all with a sure swift skill and easy grace. The quick and deadly manual of loading, sighting, and firing a rifle became an automatic action. The lives of every one of them might depend on it in those perilous moments that came so suddenly in the violent life of the border.

Girls were nimble-fingered with woof and warp on the clanking-timbered looms that made the warm stout homespun cloth of their go-to-meeting clothes. Butter, soap, and sugar making, cooking on an open fireplace or baking in out-door ovens, swingling flax and carding wool, and the molding of candles and bullets were some of the courses in which they soon qualified with high honors. They were happy making their own world, busy with making and mending or caring for the gentle or rambunctious farm animals that were almost members of the household. They provided in wise ways for the needs of tomorrow.

Growing Daniel looked forward with pleasure to the changing seasons that brought in the full or lean years with spring plowing and planting, summer hoeing, and autumn gathering. He watched the little corn blades thrust up, grow tall, and wave great arching green banners and tasseled plumes to the fierce sun, until the long full ears turned hard and yellow as gold. Then the reaping and mowing and gathering into barns with the sharp frosty nights turning the oak and maples into red and yellow glory. The hickory, walnut, and butternut trees rained down meaty plunder on frolicsome young gatherers. After that there was time for hunting in the leaf-bare woods and jollifications and feasting when the hunters brought in a fat turkey, deer, or b'ar.

Rarely wayfaring strangers stopped at the farm, were sized up shrewdly,

and if they had a godfearing look were welcomed to an abundant hospitality, or were passed on to the next settlement if they looked mean and ornery. Being good members of the Quaker faith, the Boone family gave and took among themselves and their neighbors with an easy kindness that brought a quiet sweetness to the stress and strain of heavy tasks. Out of the ponderous Bible they daily read and listened and believed, striving to walk with a wise and gentle God in love and truth.

So Daniel Boone grew lean and strong with his toes in the good black dirt, with the ring of the anvil in his ears, strong and sure-handed with tools and guns, and his head as clear and cool as the hillside spring above his cabin home.

Father and Mother Boone with their eleven children were an average-sized American family of that day, but it was as plain as the nose on your face that they were soon going to need more elbow room and plenty of it. They were already up against the steep backs of the Allegheny Mountains, and so when stories came back from movers who had drifted south about the beautiful lands in the Virginia valley and farther down into North Carolina, it sounded good to the Boones.

The clan talked it over and figured it out; some were agin it but most were for it. So they harnessed their broad-backed horses to the blue Conestoga wagons that were built as stout and graceful as ships. They filled them with the lovely hand-shaped tools, simple furniture, and the hand-woven woolen and linen

clothes. The women put on their sunbonnets and shawls and climbed aboard and the men of the tribe of Boone loaded their rifles and mounted good horse-flesh. They waved their broad hats and fired off their guns with a cheer and slowly drove off with their dogs and cattle toward the Southwest, looking back wistfully at the old home as they rode over the hill.

They crossed the Potomac at Harpers Ferry and moved through the Shenandoah valley, grazing their flocks and herds on the lush grass and hunting and fishing in the abundant forests and rivers. The land was more beautiful than they or anyone else who has not seen it could dream. It was like the stories in the Bible they knew so well, of the wanderings of God's chosen people and of Abraham in the land of Canaan. They came out of the western end of Virginia into North Carolina where, in the valley of the Yadkin, they found a land so fair that they wanted to go no farther. Squire Boone picked out an ample slice of this earthly paradise and called it home.

Bear, buffalo, deer, and all the rest of four-footed America played and roamed in the valley. All the lovely wings of America flashed in the woods. Friendly Indians sometimes came out of the western forest to barter and visit and depart into the unknown forest world. So Daniel stepped out from his boyhood into the kingdom of a man in a world almost as new as Genesis.

ALEXANDRIA on the Potomac River was the busiest port in all the colonies. Out of Alexandria sailed deep-laden British merchant ships, their holds filled with fragrant tobacco, corn, bacon, beaver skins, and all the wealth of the great plantations of cavalier Virginia. From London they brought back English gold and silver plate and the latest finery and fashions. Virginia was the proud high-stepping peacock of the royal colonies.

Just now Alexandria's streets were gay with banners and red-coated troops of His Majesty, King George the Third, marching to the quick shrill music of fife and drum. The grand invincible General Braddock had come to Virginia to lead a victorious expedition and drive the encroaching French from British soil for-

ever. The planters were giving him a sample of exuberant Virginia hospitality. All the chivalry of the near-by counties was riding down to Alexandria on thoroughbred horses. The Peytons and the Randolphs and the Lewises were riding in to give the conquering general an Old Dominion welcome. There were elegant banquets with mountains of food, and stately formal balls where the gay Virginia beauties danced and coquetted with the entranced English officers.

The fate of the log fort, which the miserable French had built at the junction of the Allegheny and Monongahela on His British Majesty's domain, was a foregone conclusion. After pleasant weeks of hospitable delay, the leisurely expedition got under way up the Potomac valley. They marched to the newly built Fort Cumberland where they met the colonial troops and wagon-trains that would clear the way for their grand parade through the forest.

Among the one hundred North Carolina riflemen marching under Captain Hugh Waddell was young Daniel Boone, taking care of the wagons and the blacksmithing. There was a young Virginia colonel of just Boone's age with

General Braddock. He irritated the general exceedingly with advice about backwoods fighting. All the more so because he knew whereof he spoke. He had been surveying all through the wild country and at the age of twenty-two had done his share of backwoods fighting with both French and Indians. The young colonel who disagreed with the old general was George Washington. He held just about the same opinion of the British as the general did of the Americans. So these three, the British general, the Virginia colonel, and the young backwoodsman, Braddock, Washington, and Boone, marched on through the all but impenetrable forest to strange destinies.

Washington was literally in a fever at the slow progress. Three miles a day was all they could make in bad places. The forest had to be cleared and the road built as they went. When the French and Indians heard that they were within ten miles of the fort, they began to lose all hope of holding out. But at the last moment, a Captain Beaujeau dressed and painted himself like an Indian, ran to where the gloomy Indian warriors were encamped, made a rousing speech, and got them under way to meet the British advance. By afternoon they had invested the woods of Turtle Creek ravine and were pouring in lead at the bright target of the British Red Coats. The charges of the British toward the hidden enemy ended in such terrible slaughter that even the heroic officers could not stem the retreat which turned into a panic by nightfall. Gallant Braddock's last words as he lay mortally wounded were: "We shall know better next time."

Colonel Washington wrote to his mother an account of the battle: "The Virginia troops showed a great deal of bravery, and were nearly all killed; for I believe out of three companies that were there, scarcely thirty men are left alive. . . . The dastardly behaviour of those they call regulars exposed all others, that were inclined to do their duty, to almost certain death; and, at last, in despite of all the efforts of the officers to the contrary, they ran, as sheep pursued by dogs,

and it was impossible to rally them. . . . I luckily escaped without a wound, though I had four bullets through my coat, and two horses shot under me."

Days later the broken fragments of Braddock's once-gay regiment staggered into Fort Cumberland. They had marched over Braddock's new-made grave to hide it from the Indians. Daniel could take care of himself in the backwoods fashion, and so he rode home in his whole skin to the Yadkin valley remembering horrible pictures of men dying in agony by the dark forest trail.

WHEN DANIEL came back to the Boone's farm in the Yadkin valley, he up and married his Irish sweetheart, Rebecca Bryan, whose family had settled in the valley near them. There was a hilarious shindig with the Carolina fiddles shaking down the moon. When the logs were all cut for the house-raising, the neighbors for miles around took a hand. By sundown they stuck a pine tree on the ridgepole of a brand new cabin in the clearing and ate and danced till morning. The young Boones moved in, happy and hard-working, and in a few years had a going farm and two fine boys, all busy with crops and cattle and snake fences.

[2 1]

Late on a night of clouded moon, a runner crossed the cabin clearing like a moving shadow and rapped softly once and again at the cabin door. Boone passed the whispered message to Rebecca: "The Indians are on the warpath and are coming down the valley." In the darkness Boone saddled the horses and took his loaded rifle while Rebecca gathered a few clothes and some food. The children moved quickly and silently, and soon they were all mounted and riding hard through the night toward Fort Dobbs, the log fort where every family rushed for safety when the news of Indian raiders came at an hour's warning. The white families knew only too well how the fierce red warriors would surround the cabins just before dawn, terrible in the ghastly white and black war paint, fearsome images of violent death that haunted the dreams of every border family.

Nearing the fort the Boones met other refugees with stories of frightful Indian vengeance. Five savages had hacked in the door of one cabin, desperately wounding the man; but his wife with an ax had killed three as they came singly through the door, and had in the same manner dispatched two more who had climbed down the chimney. There were hundreds of such stark tales around the border forts and settlements.

The fort compound was already crowded when the Boones arrived and the stream of refugees increased daily. Food and even water were scarce. As it became clear that the fort could not hold all of the fleeing settlers, it was decided that some would have to go back to the safety of the Virginia settlements. Since the Boones were among the last arrivals, they must move on. So the little cavalcade of refugees wound its way sadly north to Culpeper, Virginia.

Having lost all their worldly possessions, Daniel was glad to accept a friendly offer of a job as wagoner on a tobacco plantation and drive slow teams hauling great wagons loaded with the pungent leaves down to the market at Fairfax. Back and forth on the rough roads and at the bustling taverns, there was news aplenty of the Indian wars. Daniel's heart burned as he listened to how the Indian raid on Fort Dobbs had been beaten back with heavy losses to the Indians who had abandoned the attack, and how Fort Prince George on the Savannah had driven off the Cherokees, and the rumors of the long-drawn-out siege of Fort Loudon, the stone fort with cannon far down the Tennessee, the farthest outpost in the wilderness. And now came news of a great army of regulars including the kilted Scotch Highlanders with their bagpipes, who were being sent out by South Carolina to break the power of the Cherokee tribes and free the border from the Indian terror once and for all.

When Daniel heard that Captain Waddell, under whom he had served before, was calling for volunteers for a regiment of Carolina backwoodsmen, he could stand it no longer. These boys were his people who really *knew* how to fight Indians, and when they were through he knew the farms on the Yadkin would be safe again. So he was saying a choking farewell to Rebecca and the youngsters and riding off with his own equipment on a fine Virginia horse to join the army.

The backwoods militiamen were a rough, tough breed of undisciplined adventurers out on their own looking for a hand-to-hand sniping fight with the red varmints. They were fierce fighters in their own way, critical of their officers, quarrelsome and boisterous, and when the fun and excitement wore off they became disgusted with hardship and starvation and rode back to their homes whether their short-term enlistment had expired or no. They rode back on lean horses to the cabin in the clearing, to an affectionate welcome from the faithful wife, a small army of devoted children, and an uproarious barking of hound dogs, swearing they were done with soldiering for good.

It was long months before young Daniel came back from the Tennessee expedition, a lean veteran of many fights. He told his wide-eyed boys how they had followed the Indians down the Tennessee, burning their towns and destroying whole tribes, and how the army had marched into an Indian ambuscade so desperate that for an hour it had looked like another Braddock's defeat, till the Carolina backwoodsmen with their deadly rifles had made it too hot for the hidden Cherokees. The regulars had been able to get out of the narrow defile and retreat to Charleston.

✓ Here is an account of the destruction of an Indian village, as told by a backwoodsman who was present, in the *Autobiography of David Crockett*: "We took them all prisoners that came out to us in this way; but I saw some warriors run into a house, until I counted forty-six of them. We pursued them until we got near the house, when we saw a squaw sitting in the door, and she placed her feet against the bow she had in her hand, and then took an arrow, and raising her feet she drew with all her might and let fly at us and she killed a man, whose name I believe was Moore. He was a lieutenant and his death so enraged us all that she was fired on, and had at least twenty balls blown through her. This was the first man I ever saw killed with a bow and arrow. We now shot them like dogs; and then set the house on fire, and burned it up with the forty-six warriors in it. I recollect seeing a boy who was shot down near the house. His arm and thigh were broken, and he was so near the burning house that the grease was stewing out of him. In this situation he was still trying to crawl along; but not a murmur escaped him though he was only about twelve years old. So sullen is the Indian when his dander is up that he had sooner die than make a noise, or ask for quarters."

The Boones now rode back to the beloved Yadkin valley where they had started life together on the prosperous little farm that had promised so much. They looked forward with joy to taking up again the free peaceful life in the quiet valley. But they soon found that things were not the same. Many new settlers were coming into the valley and it seemed that almost overnight a new cabin had sprung up on every hill. Now the buffalo were gone and the deer and bear were hard to find or shoot. Things were different—getting so crowded that there was hardly elbow room. The great landlords were demanding costly land titles and bringing in slave labor so that it was a disgrace for a white man to work with his hands. Law sharks and horse thieves were plentiful.

So the growing family of Boones began moving farther into the West, first one cabin and then another, until they were back in the shadow of blue mountains that kept calling: "Come on over." Daniel's fall hunting trips became longer. He was counting on the forest more and more for food, and on the profits from beaver and other furs more than from crops or herds.

He would take little nine-year-old Jamie along and teach him the secret ways of the deep woods. At the end of a day's hard hunting, of skinning and butchering the kill, they would lie on the fragrant hemlock boughs with their feet to the fire and talk over the day's adventures until they dozed off into cat's sleep, their rifles within quick reach.

In the fall of 1765 Boone with a party of "long hunters" rode south along Indian trails through Georgia deep into Florida, coming back empty-handed after four months but with a hatful of tall stories of alligators and the dismal swamp where they would have starved but for the friendly Seminole Indians. Boone told Rebecca of a place called Pensacola, where he had traded skins for a house and lot where they could go and live. But Rebecca for once put her foot down so hard that Daniel never mentioned it again. When he wanted to set out with the Yadkin boys on a long overland trek to the Mississippi River land, Rebecca again went on the rampage. He sadly gave in, saying that she didn't seem ever to get used to being a long hunter's wife. But come the fall he would be going on the winter fur hunt.

This time he traveled west with a couple of cronies, out between the Cumberland and the Allegheny Mountains and down the Big Sandy River to the Ohio. They were snowed in at the salt licks, where the big game herds came to lick the salty ground near the mineral springs. It was a fine winter's hunt and Boone returned, not knowing he had actually been in the promised land of Kentucky. Mysterious Kentucky beyond the southwest-lying mountain ranges and valleys! He knew that the Clinch and Powell Rivers flowed down their steep valleys to the mighty Tennessee that disappeared into the West. He knew that the Kanawha flowed out of the Alleghenies and into the broad Ohio, that perilous

Indian-infested highway to the Mississippi. Was there a land of plenty lying somewhere between these mighty rivers—a garden of Eden unknown to man, teeming with a fabulous abundance of fat land, of fish and game? He had known a man who talked of these things long ago when he served in Braddock's army. He had often dreamed of a way, some river trail or hidden pass that would lead surely over the mountains to the unknown plains. It might be the gateway to a new America, a fabulous western world with a destiny of glory like the towering storm clouds in a fiery sunset.

Sometimes down the lone valley where the Boone cabin snuggled, trailed the long hunters coming from the Indian country; wild, dark, careless men with their tall talk of the free life among the Indians beyond the mountains—of the outlandish tribes, Cherokees, Shawnees, Choctaws, Creeks, Chickasaws, and Casawabas—of their great towns of Chota, Chillicothe, Keowee, Mackachunk, and Tallaposa—of their fierce chiefs and emperors, Logan, Cornstalk, Dragging Canoe, Red Shoes, Little Carpenter, and Oconatosta.

Coming back to the settlements in the spring with their fur packs, they sold them by weight to the agents of the great fur companies, spent their money on high times, and were looked down on by the sober settlers as shiftless and traipsin'. Then in the fall with whisky and beads and a few supplies they rode mysteriously away toward the Indian country.

One day there stopped at the Boone farm a strange lean trapper. Daniel eyed him keenly for a few slow moments and then roared out: "Why, if it ain't Finley who I ain't seen in a coon's age." It was Finley, the trapper whom he had known in the old campaign days under Braddock. They sat late into the night talking of old times and remembering stirring scenes. Finley ran on about the good land over the mountains, the fat valley soil, the fair rivers, the vast herds of buffalo and game, a settler's and hunter's paradise. He knew the trails and hidden passes into mysterious Kentucky.

All the old mover's itch, that had pulled the feet westward since the first white man beached a boat on American shores, took hold of Daniel's insides. There were days of talk, for Rebecca took a deal of persuading. "It will be a hard lone time for me, Daniel Boone, not knowing if your bones are rotting in the black woods in the winter nights with the snow piled high and your empty chair every night by the fire, and no thanks to you, wild Finley, for the tongue of yours with your high fine lies that will be leading him to a bad end."

[28]

But this time Daniel had the last word, with how she was among her own people, and the Boones and the Bryans would be helping the boys take care of the farm and herself, and himself coming back in the spring with a bale of pelts worth a fortune. This time he was going. So they were saying good-by to the Boones and the Bryans and the Calloways before sunup and waving good-by to Rebecca at the cabin door with the boys, as six of them rode out of the valley in the thick white morning mist.

Finley's cavalcade of six horsemen rode west toward the Watauga River valley, which made a level trail winding between steep shoulders of the mountains. These westward-flowing streams were the only highways through the mountains into the West. To attempt to cross the innumerable ranges would have been a task so slow and tedious as to be almost impossible. Following along the narrow little valley, they soon came out on the south fork of the Holston. This noble river wound through a wider valley of thrilling beauty. They followed down stream to a narrow defile and by stiff climbing passed over the Clinch Mountains and River to the Powell valley.

They were moving through some of the most beautiful country in the world that few white men had ever seen. It was spring, before the leaves were out, and the noble forms of the piling blue ranges stood out in the clear air like sculpture for eternity. When rain and mist slowed down the going, they stretched by the camp fire after the day's march and dried their buckskin leggings, as the shadows danced strangely among the great trees. They were advancing directly onto the mighty wall of the Cumberlands where Finley said they would find a passage through. They climbed easy slopes, stopped, looked back on immense vistas, and went on into new country. Coming down out of the great pass they followed the Cumberland River through wild and savage gorges.

They came now into easy rolling country with low hills where a hunter could range at will. The streams were plentiful and the soil black with richness. Huge black buffalo thundered down to the salt licks or grunted in the juicy canebrakes. The underbrush was thick with game, and they feasted on the fat wild turkey that ran under the horses' feet.

Excited and buoyant they rode northward, coming to the Rockcastle River winding among mountains of fantastic beauty. They kept on north through open country that was a settler's dream of plenty. Soon they were wandering along the fabled banks of the Kentucky. Following the game trails and the wide buffalo streets they discovered the Upper and Lower Blue Licks, the strange mineral springs where the buffalo and deer came eagerly to lick the salty ground.

[31]

Having seen no trace of human beings in this Garden of Eden, they forgot the frontier vigilance of Indian fighters, but not for long. As Boone and John Stewart were emerging from a canebrake near the Kentucky River, a dozen Shawnee warriors sprang on them so suddenly that they were captured and bound before they could fire a shot. In this sudden and dismal change of fortune Boone's dauntless spirit rose, and his nonchalance and apparent friendliness made the Indians feel that he was really glad to be captured. After hunting with them for a week, their captors were so completely off guard that Boone and Stewart were able to slip out from their blankets beside the snoring Indians one night and escape to their old camp, only to find that their friends had gone without leaving any sign of when or where. Again Daniel's singing spirit rallied. The two could take care of themselves; they knew all the tricks of the wilderness. So they lived from day to day cautiously spying out the land.

Once from a hilltop they spotted two horsemen riding across an open valley. They lay in ambush looking over their rifle sights. Then with the suddenness of an Indian surprise Daniel recognized his own brother. With masterly woodcraft, Squire Boone and a companion had been able to trail and guess and follow Daniel's path across four hundred miles of trackless mountain wilderness and find him.

Much encouraged and with plenty of supplies, they set about systematic hunting for furs, going off in pairs for the day's hunt and meeting at sundown at their hidden camp. One night, Boone's companion failed to show up. When they could find no trace of him the third man started back for the settlements alone. The two brothers looked at each other across the camp fire that night, alone in a hostile land. They were well-equipped; they were experienced woodsmen. It was foolish to go back without fur bales, and above all the love of the wilderness was in their blood and bones. So they built a hidden cabin against the

cold and trapped and skinned furs all the long white winter. When spring came the fur piles were high and the ammunition low. So they planned for Squire to take back the pelts and Daniel's love to the folks, and he would stay on till Squire returned with more supplies. If it all worked out they would have another long hunt the next year.

Boone stood on a hilltop under a giant walnut tree with his long-barreled rifle across his arm, waving his broad-brimmed hat. He could still see Squire crossing a stream and waving a last good-by before he vanished into the heavy timber. As Boone went back to the cabin a terrible loneliness came over him—a longing for home, Rebecca and the children, friends, and the sound of human voices. He had been a fool not to return with Squire. He cooked his lonesome supper, a strip of venison broiled on the iron ramrod of his rifle. As he sat gazing into the fire he fought a black despair and the primeval nameless fear of darkness that came with the night.

Next day the clear-shining sun rose over the vast land like high-calling trumpets of glory. The splendor and the brightness came upon his spirit like the rushing of mighty wings, and the voice of mighty thunderings: "Enter into a promised land such as no man has known, a new born creation all your own; drink deep, O Daniel, of the mysterious wine of the wilderness."

A new sense of freedom and power possessed him as he ranged over the long hills and followed shrewdly the secret waterways. He was the only freeman in all the western world, like Man himself in the Beginning of Things. Hunter and hunted, he measured his woodcraft against the forest prowlers. Chased to the edge of a high cliff and cornered by Indians, he leaped into a tree-top and so away like the wild rabbit. He hid under waterfalls and swung across streams on wild grapevines. He lay in the canebrake and sang to himself an old Virginia ballad with a rousing refrain. He laughed to think of himself as a jack rabbit dodging

the Shawnees in the laurel bushes, a red fox of the canebrakes with a fat part-ridge in his teeth, a lean young wolf of the wilderness trotting over the long hills sniffing the four winds of Kentucky or nosing down the valleys, finding the ways to the salt licks and the sweet waters flowing under the stars. When he won a hard fight with an extra-big bear he felt full of boast and brag and carved on a tree in his own personal spelling: "D. BOON cilled a bar," with the date, and was very pleased.

Faithful Squire came again after many weeks, and what a meeting it was! As Daniel listened to news from the forgotten world it all came back to him, the old affections and memories, till he hardly knew which life was a dream and which real. They spent another winter trapping, and again Squire rode off to the settlements with rich bales. He returned to the old cabin, but with the coming of spring they broke camp and made a voyage of exploration down the Cumber-land River. As they came through the Gap and looked behind them toward Ken-tucky, Daniel heard voices out of the sunset calling: "Come back soon, come back to Kentucky, Daniel Boone."

They crossed into Virginia through the Cumberland Gap, into the Powell valley where they were taken by surprise by an Indian war party and robbed of everything. After two years of hunting in the wilderness, the Boones came home with only the shirts on their backs—and lucky at that. It was the way of the wilderness.

The Yadkin settlement was all astir over the return of Daniel Boone. He sat at the cabin hearth with the children on his knees, listening to Rebecca saying: "So you're back, Daniel Boone, like a banshee out of the West and me looking long into the sunset, month in and month out, these two weary lonely years, hungry for the sight of you. Any other woman would have taken a man twice over but me, with the aching love for you in my heart and never closing my eyes

[36]

of a winter's night without a tear and a prayer that the good Lord would be sending his angels to keep watch and ward over you day and night in the cold and the rain."

So Daniel patiently worked the small farm on the Yadkin and talked of the wonderful land of Kentucky to the eager listening neighbors. It sounded good to restless land-hungry men ready to move on. It was the call of the golden West forever saying: "More freedom and good fortune across the mountains under the new moon seen over your left shoulder."

Soon Daniel was the leader and guide of a group of families getting ready to leave, selling out, packing up, rounding up the babies, children, horses, dogs, cows, and pigs—ready to shove off, hit the trail, start all over again from scratch with a rifle, ax, plow, and Bible. So there was a gypsy farewell through the tears —good-by dear hearts, old homes—good-by the past. A bright dawn saw the cavalcade gaily riding toward the blue battlements of the unknown, plunging into the rough steep mountain country.

At last they were making camp in the Powell valley. It was the rendezvous where they were to await a party of forty more colonists from the Bryan settlement, to make together the final push through Cumberland Gap into the plains of plenty. Also a famous border clan of Russell was to join them there, and Daniel sent his eldest boy Jamie down the valley a day's journey to tell Captain Russell that they were ready and waiting. When Jamie did not get back the second night it was all right—Jamie was eighteen and could take care of himself. But the next day two exhausted men came in with the terrible news of an Indian attack. Riding to the scene Boone found six scalped corpses, among them those of the two boys, Jamie and Russell's son Henry.

The wilderness had taken its terrible vengeance on the hunters who had pried into its secrets. It was as though the ancient gods of the forest had taken for sacrifice the eldest sons of its violators. When the Bryan party arrived the spirit of the expedition was broken. The woods were sinister with sudden death. Grimly Boone urged them on. With his heart set ever westward it was hard to turn back. The Boones spent a lonely winter with grief and hunger in an abandoned cabin in the Clinch valley.

All along the border ranges the storm was gathering. Episodes of violence and murder were fanning flames of hate and vengeance into a general war. The Indians were sure the whites would be driven back over the mountains.

A surveying party had gone down the Ohio River and was camped at the Falls. Unless someone could warn them and guide them they would never return alive. Boone and his friend, Michael Stoner, took the job, went through four hundred miles of trackless wilderness, found the surveyors, and brought them unharmed through hostile Indian country, covering eight hundred miles in sixty days.

The backwoods settlers were fleeing into the border forts with bloody tales of massacre, torture, and desperate escapes. Boone had volunteered to go with Colonel Lewis to join Lord Dunsmore's army going down the Ohio against the Indian chieftain, Cornstalk. But men of experience with knowledge of the country were needed to protect the widely separated forts and settlements along the border. For this kind of fighting Boone was especially qualified. He was appointed lieutenant and then captain, and his quick marches and sudden attacks broke up and routed the Indian war parties with such energy that with the defeat of Cornstalk by Lewis at Point Pleasant the border was cleared and the Cherokees driven far down the Tennessee. The quiet mild-mannered captain was famous all through the mountains for his cool courage and skill as an Indian fighter. His work finished, he took his discharge from the army and went for a long hunt through the Gap and down the Kentucky River.

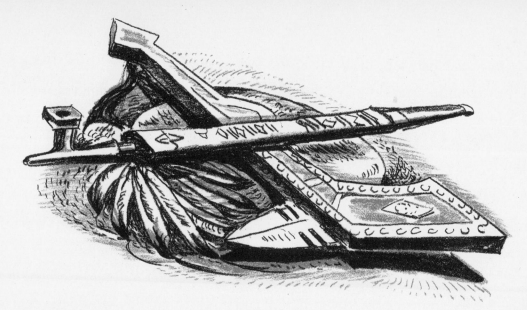

OVER THE OHIO valley linger the long shadows of Logan and Corn-stalk and Dragging Canoe, of old Oconatosta, of Atta Culla Culla, and Moluntha and Black Fish. The splendid copper-gleaming images of the dreaded Indian chieftains emerged suddenly out of the dark green forest background. In their white buffalo robes they stand tall and glittering in claw necklaces and wampum and copper armlets. From their high crests and roached scalp-locks dangle eagle feathers. They come to the solemn councils with their war axes, turkey-feather fans, hatchet pipes; and they barter away the forests for corn whisky and a red shirt, or striking their war hatchets into the ground hurl death and defiance to the treacherous pale faces.

The wise old prophet-chiefs saw their destiny in the sky; they knew their fate was the doom of the buffalo. They saw the last tribes driven like mists down the mountain valleys before the brightness of the pale-faced gods. The axes and arrows of the stone age were useless against the deadly guns and fiery poisons of the white man. Amid their burning villages and the awful butcheries and sicken-ing betrayals of friends and foes, they met the personal tragedy of violent death with a serene indifference.

[39]

Fragments of Indian speeches were written down by white men who listened at the council fires. They have the pathos and solemn grandeur of the last testament of a doomed race.

* "There was a time when our forefathers owned this great island. Their seas extended from the rising to the setting sun. The Great Spirit had made it for the use of the Indians. All this He had done for His children because He loved them.

"But an evil day came upon us. Your forefathers crossed the great water, and landed on this island. Their numbers were small. They found friends, not enemies. They told us they had fled from their country for fear of wicked men and had come here to enjoy their religion. They asked for a small seat. We took pity on them, granted their request, and they sat down among us. We gave them corn and meat. They gave us poison in return.

"The white people had now found our country. Tidings were carried back and more came among us. Yet we did not fear them. We took them to be friends. They called us brothers. We believed them, and gave them a large seat. At length their numbers had greatly increased. They wanted more land. They wanted our country. Our eyes were opened, and our minds became uneasy. Wars took place. Indians were hired to fight against Indians and many of our people were destroyed. They also brought strong liquor among us. It was strong and powerful and has slain thousands. You have now become a great people and we have scarcely a place left to spread our blankets. You have got our country, but are not satisfied. You want to force your religion on us.

"You say there is but one way to worship and serve the Great Spirit. If there is but one religion, why do you white people differ so much about it? Why not all agreed, as you can all read the book?

"We do not understand these things."

---

* Selected from "Reply to a Missionary Agent," by Red Jacket, of the Senecas. *American Memory*, edited by Henry Beston (Farrar and Rinehart, New York).

II TRANSYLVANIA

ALL PIONEERS did not wear buckskin breeches and coonskin caps. There was Colonel Richard Henderson, or Judge Henderson, for he was both, who had come out of Virginia into the Carolinas and had got on in the world exceedingly well by way of the law. He conceived the shrewd notion of turning Kentucky into a real estate development. Being a man with a gift for getting things done, he formed a company for the purpose of acquiring about two million acres west of the Cumberland Mountains from the Cherokee tribes who, although they had no papers to prove it, had possessed the land from im-memorial time.

[42]

The Transylvania Company was the pretty name of the colonel's enterprise. Henderson engaged Daniel Boone to get the Indians together in the right frame of mind for the big deal, after which he was to blaze a trail or rough road into the new domain so that settlers could make their way into the country and buy virgin acres from the Company for homes and farms.

So Boone took the news of Mr. Henderson's plan for a big powwow to the Cherokee chiefs, and it was debated in long orations by the council fires. The tribes would meet the white men at Sycamore Shoals on the Watauga.

When the Transylvania Company arrived at the Shoals with ten wagon-loads of ribbons and mirrors, red shirts and discarded muskets, twelve thousand eager Cherokee warriors were waiting in their paint, eagle feathers, and white buffalo robes. After the visiting and feasting and long speeches and persuading, Little Carpenter and some of the other chiefs signed away their tribal hunting grounds in spite of the anger of Dragging Canoe, who fiercely denounced the bitter folly. Said a departing chieftain grimly to Boone: "Brother, it is a good land we have sold you but you will find it hard to hold."

Boone went back at once to Long Island on the Holston. Thirty men with axes, guns, horses, dogs, and Negro slaves all provided by Mr. Henderson, were waiting for him to cut the wilderness road to Kentucky. Colonel Richard Calloway and Daniel's old companion in adventure, Michael Stoner, were along; and there was an observing young man named Felix Walker, who took the trouble to write down what happened every day and so wrote his name in history. He was badly wounded by an Indian bullet before he reached Kentucky. Strangely enough there were two women, Boone's married daughter Sarah and a Negress.

The Cherokees had buried the war hatchet and Daniel was ready to use all his knowledge of the new country to connect up the Indian trails, the Warriors' Trace, and the buffalo paths into one trail for horses, and later for wagons, out to the Kentucky River where the capital of the Transylvania empire was to be established.

Everyone was full of golden dreams and excitement for the great adventure. They cut their way through the wild country by hard work, making slow progress day by day. They felt secure from the dreaded Indian raids, till one gray dawn when they leaped to their guns, dodging the fire of an Indian surprise; two were wounded, one fatally, before they could drive off the Shawnee war party. But for Boone's iron courage and determination they would have turned back. The constant fear of suddenly getting a bullet in the back from a hidden enemy made the tired axemen want to quit and go home.

But the worst was really over, for now they were coming out into more open country where they saw the great herds of deer and buffalo trooping to the salt licks. Game was so abundant in this untouched wilderness that everyone was soon well-fed and happy. As they came down the beautiful Kentucky River they took it easy, and when they reached Otter Creek the tired axemen quickly knocked together a few cabins and called it a job. They went off gaily to get the first cut at the land and lay out their fortune in claims, or kill the larger game so recklessly and wastefully that soon a man had to walk twenty miles to find a deer or bear, the meat on which their lives depended.

Boone could not get them to work on the permanent fort he knew must be built before the Indians struck again and the families began to pour over the Wilderness Road from the settlements. He had sent a letter back to Henderson telling of the Indian attacks along the new trail and urging Henderson to come with men and supplies. The colonel had started, but it was impossible to get the wagons over the rough roads and he finally loaded pack horses with the supplies and rode safely into the discouraged camp on April 1st, 1776. No time must be lost in building the fort to protect themselves and the coming settlers. Together the colonel and Boone selected the best site for the fort and carefully laid out the cabins, walls, and corner-towers. Gangs of men began the heavy labor of planting rows of upright logs side by side to form the outer palisade against which the inner cabins were built.

Mr. Henderson now called on the four settlements of the new territory to elect representatives to meet at an Assembly in Boonesborough and make laws for his kingdom of Transylvania. On the appointed day the representatives rode in from Harrodsburg, St. Asaphs, and Boiling Spring and sat down in the shade of the great elm where Mr. Henderson from an imposing platform read the most elegant speech the old forests had ever heard. It was the grandfather of all the elegant speechifying that was to be made in Kentucky. The delegates were much impressed but they made reservations. It sounded all right, but would it work? However, they signed on the dotted line an agreement for a proprietary government which left about everything to the Company.

But it was the wrong time to start a proprietary government in America, for within a week the news of the Battle of Lexington had echoed over the mountains. The high prices at Mr. Henderson's store in the fort were getting even higher, but it was not until the Transylvania Company raised the land prices from twenty to fifty shillings a hundred acres that the settlers got riled enough to send their vehement objections to the Virginia legislature.

Mr. Henderson had made a forehanded attempt to persuade the Continental Congress to admit Transylvania as a state into the new government, but democratic-minded gentlemen like Mr. Jefferson and Samuel Adams and Benjamin Franklin were cool about proprietary government. The Transylvania Company later came to an end when the Virginia Assembly divided Transylvania into counties of the State of Virginia, but Mr. Henderson was given 200,000 acres for opening up the country.

[45]

Right now Boonesborough was having a big celebration over the battle of Lexington, for they knew the Americans across the mountains were fighting for independence. Just as New England was starting on her own to make an independent nation of contrivers and inventors, of munition-makers and sermon-preachers, so over the mountains to the West another America was making its own kind of democracy, making war with rifle and ax and plow, wiping out the Indians and buffalo, destroying the great forests, and raising up green armies of tall corn in the valley bottoms. One was to be a nation of money-counters and machines, the other a barefooted rail-splitting, haranguing, horse-racing democracy of lean mule-drivers and land-poor, camp-meeting corn-huskers. One stood on the shoulders of black slavery, the other on wage slavery. They were to stand against each other in war and in politics, land against dollars, the few against the many, and yet to be bound together by invisible hands of indestructible union.

So Mr. Henderson fades out of the picture with Transylvania and English dominion and the Indian and the buffalo. But Mr. Henderson's big idea remains a part of the American dream—the big Company, the big Profits, industrial Empires and Billionaires. Mr. Henderson and Daniel Boone, depending on each other, stood for two ways of life, two forces that pull and tug and say: "What price Democracy?"

After the delegates to the first Assembly had ridden back to their settlements and the fort of Boonesborough had been practically completed, they were ready for the families who were to come and make homes in this little island of civilization in the empty vastness of the forests. Boone went to bring Rebecca and the children and to escort and protect the supplies of salt and powder that would accompany the immigrant families now eager to settle in the storied paradise. Men were riding over the wilderness road who would play immortal parts in the primitive dramas of the new country—handsome reckless young Simon Kenton, George Rogers Clark, Benjamin Logan, the Bentons, the Bryans, the Randolphs, and many other first families of the Kentucky to come. Parties were arriving with their flocks and herds, cows and pigs, innumerable towheaded children and shirt-tail boys.

Plows were cutting the forest loam in fresh-made clearings. Spinning wheels hummed and cradle songs drifted across the drowsing river. Girls brought water from the spring and the young men shaved and washed behind their ears. Mr. Henderson's new store did a thriving business.

Boonesborough was starting to grow up.

III · BOONESBOROUGH

THE LOG walls of Boonesborough were twelve feet high. According to Benjamin Franklin it took two axmen six minutes to fell a fourteen-inch-thick pine, which made three sixteen-foot palisades. These were sharpened to a point at one end and set close against each other in a four-foot trench. Inside, a firing-board six feet from the ground ran around the entire stockade. The Boonesborough fort was a rectangle of log walls, or palisade, one hundred seventy by two hundred fifty feet, with four corner-towers and two heavy log gates. Thirty cabins within the stockade were built into the outside wall. It was separated from the surrounding forest by a stump-dotted clearing. When the riflemen inside were at their firing posts, no enemy could cross this no-man's-land alive. Only cannon could demolish their wilderness citadel.

They never knew these days whether the laurel bushes hid a dozen or hundreds of the prowling Indian varmints watching for a chance to make a deadly shot. One day the lookout saw several redskins crawling out into the open. In the excitement Boone and his men made a dash for them across the clearing only to find too late that they had been caught in an ambush. Boone went down with a bullet in his ankle and a huge savage swinging a hatchet down at his defenseless skull, but a point-blank shot from Simon Kenton's rifle dropped the Indian in his tracks. In the running fight to reach the stockade Kenton managed to carry the disabled Boone to safety. Simon Kenton was a young wildcat with nine lives for the Indians to catch and tie to the back of a frightened horse for a mad ride among the tearing branches.

Then again two hundred Shawnees surrounded the clearing and poured lead into the stockade for two days. The fifty riflemen at the portholes clipped every redskin that showed an inch from cover, while the women molded bullets and loaded hot rifle barrels. Boonesborough was having its baptism of fire and remembering about the dark and bloody ground, hard to hold. When several parties of armed settlers came in like little armies with supplies of salt and powder, the watching Indians retreated taking news of mighty advancing troops of long-knives to the Chillicothe villages. The defenders welcomed the newcomers with boisterous joy.

A midsummer Sunday afternoon was a still, quiet time for Daniel's daughter, Jemima Boone, and Fanny and Betsy Calloway (crammed with the Lamentations of Jeremiah and the wrath of God from the Sunday morning Bible reading) to slip down the winding lazy Kentucky River in a canoe. The long afternoon drowsed on to milking time, and there were no signs of Fanny and Betsy and Jemima. "Where are the girls?" ran from cabin to cabin. The river searchers came in with bad news—they had found the empty canoe and the girls' tracks and those of five Indians on the river bank. A swift council of the best trackers figured out the rescue plan. It was a pretty sure guess that the Indians would make for their tribal village on Licking River, and the hunters knew the lay of the land.

Boone, John Floyd, and the Calloway boys started at dawn on the trail. The girls had slyly, and even under the cat-eyes of their captors, left plain signs —a broken branch or piece of ribbon. Every hour the traces grew fresher as the savages, believing they were out of reach of pursuit, became less careful and finally camped in seeming safety. It was a terrible moment for the pursuers when they crept in close. They knew that at the least suspicious sound the savages would instantly tomahawk the captives. The hunters fired together. Two Indians dropped in their tracks, and the others dived into the forest.

The awful tension and suspense had snapped like a thread. There was wild joy when the happy party came out into the Boonesborough clearing. Everyone

told the story with all the details, over and over. Three weeks later Samuel Henderson and his sweetheart Elizabeth Calloway came to Justice Boone who solemnly performed the ceremony of the first marriage in Kentucky. Later Flanders Calloway married Daniel's beloved daughter Jemima, and Fanny Calloway married young John Holder, who was to make a great name as an Indian fighter.

The life of a pioneer family was a comic-tragic drama of struggle and violence. Each one had many stories. The lives of these movers on the Wilderness Road and forest settlers were a rough and violent saga full of lights and shadows, sweet and bitter as the wild persimmon, rough and tough as the shag-barked hickories, fierce and tender as the tall waving corn of the valleys.

Boone's story was the story of a whole people. It had all their griefs and tragedies and restless longings and rich half-fulfilled dreams, all their ranging freedom and mortal bondages. It rang with the roaring laughter and boisterous fun; it was dark with the unfathomable silent anguishes by new-made graves; it was full of lost hopes and dreams of grandeur. Through it rushed the winds and the voices of the valley, the vast Ohio valley. Through the story runs the clamor of distant voices, of the generations springing up from the bottom lands, the fat corn lands, saying: "We are the nation of the valley, the tall corn-fed, hog-fed sons of the West. We make our own destiny and we like it. We make our own glories and shames and we've just begun. Our songs and our dreams are made of the new moon over the dry corn shocks, of the wind in the maple groves, of the silver-weathered rails in the fence along a prairie road."

A PATTERN of fur-clad hunters and long-eared hounds and pack horses carrying iron salt-kettles, trailing among the black leafless trees, made a silhouette on the blue-white snow that lay deep over the winter world of Kentucky. They were going to French Lick to boil thousands of gallons of water at the salt springs in order that desperate Boonesborough might have the salt that kept the meat from putrefying so Boonesborough could eat and live.

In the dead of winter the salt-camp at French Lick felt safe from the Indians, whose custom was to take the war path only in the spring or summer. But one gray evening in February as Boone was coming back to camp after a long day's hunt, he was completely surprised by an ambush of four Indian warriors. He tried to run for it but in the deep snow it was useless. The Old Fox of Kentucky was caught again. They were the very Shawnees from whom he had escaped years ago on the Finley expedition. It was a tough heart-breaking moment but he had been there more than once before and had come through. Now it was a quick shift of tactics from physical action to a game of wits and bluff.

The Indians were a large war party under Chief Black Fish headed for a surprise attack on Boonesborough. Suddenly to have caught the great chief of the white men so excited them that Boone was able shrewdly to persuade them to change their plan. The silent white hunter must have turned eloquent and impressive as he stood in the midst of the savage council that was to give the tomahawk vote of life or death for the unsuspecting salt camp. Fantastic as it sounds, nevertheless the war party agreed to leave Boonesborough till the spring, when Boone promised he would arrange a peaceable moving of the settlers farther north where they might live as adopted Shawnees. For the present the Indians would return to Chillicothe with the unscalped salt-boilers as their prisoners. All this was argued out in talk and translated back and forth by a Negro named Pompey.

[5 3]

Though Boone had saved the fort on the Kentucky and the salt-camp from bloody butchery by his courage and wits alone, some of the men were bitter and resentful against him as they marched half-starved and frozen into the winter encampment of the Shawnees at Chillicothe. After a while Black Fish led a party with the white captives to Detroit to exhibit them and perhaps sell them to General Hamilton.

Detroit in 1776 was a British fort and trading post perched on the open waterway of the Great Lakes. The rich fur trade of a vast area of wild North America passed through there on the way to make fortunes in far-off King George's England. Now there was a revolution in the colonies. It would be bad for the fur business. Inside the fort the red-coated British soldiers went through their daily drill. They dreamed in their barracks of English lanes and ale houses and rosy English sweethearts.

Outside the fort the red tribes came and went at will. They traded and treated with the English soldiers and traders after their touchy quick-changing fashion. White trappers, wild and savage as the Indians, drifted in with their fur packs to swap for ammunition and to liquor up. A trader coming in with a keg of French brandy would leave town with great bales of fine furs, and a wild drunken orgy of whooping and fighting would follow. The Indians brought in from the border raids white captives, men, women, and children, as well as scalps. For these General Hamilton, the British commander, paid fixed prices in money, Indian finery, and war paint. The black faces of African Negroes mingled in the fantastic pageant. Around these wilderness outposts surged a drama of fierce passions and violent deeds.

It was a grand show-off when Black Fish's party stalked out of the forest with the great Daniel and ten of his men as captives. The whole town thrilled to see the legendary hero of the border in the flesh. Boone was as persuasive with

the British as with the Indians. He showed his commission as a captain in His British Majesty's army and told of his fictitious plan to capture Boonesborough in the spring. Hamilton was delighted with him. But when it came to selling his prisoners, Black Fish insisted that Boone was his personal property and he was not for sale, even though the general raised the price to the fabulous sum of one hundred pounds.

Boone took a long look at Detroit as he rode back into the forest with the returning Indians. It might be the last time he would ever see white faces.

The naked Indian children stared in wonder at Daniel Boone, and the lean wolf dogs snarled and snapped, not liking his strange white smell as he sat squinting at the fire in the smoky huts of Chillicothe. He was thinking his white man's thoughts as he watched the tall idle warriors and the bronze squaws grinding corn, scraping the skins, kneading the buffalo robes to make them soft. He had done very well pretending he was an Indian, pretending he was happy and satisfied, and pleasing the great chieftain Moluntha with his clever hunting. He looked wistfully at the fat Indian ponies, thinking of a dash for freedom when the right moment came. They had washed away his white blood in the river, pulled out half his hair, and painted him with strange symbols that meant he was the adopted son of the chief Black Fish. He knew by heart the strange rhythms of the mysterious ceremonial songs and dances. He was quick to share in the red laughter or laments.

One evening he came back tired from tedious labor at the salt licks to find the braves in war paint dancing to the pounding drums and shrill war chants. Sitting in his familiar place, he watched the wild frenzies rise and sway around the flickering campfires. There were five hundred warriors preparing for a surprise attack on Boonesborough. He knew how few were the defenders and that the fort was in bad repair. The whole settlement would be utterly unprepared. His hour had come and he was ready. Before dawn he slipped out like a shadow and was gone. Now again he was the hunted fox of the wilderness with the red dogs in close pursuit.

"On the 16th I departed before sunrise in the most secret manner and arrived at Boonesborough on the 20th, after a journey of one hundred and sixty miles, during which I had but one meal." Brief autobiography. How did he know the way all the four days and nights with the Shawnee pack one jump behind?

He was not so young as he used to be but tough and long-winded. When he came at last to the Ohio at full spring flood, he remembered he could not swim. It was the desperate tight spot he had known so often, but the angel of the wilderness showed him a leaky canoe stranded on a sand bar and he made a swift down-stream crossing on the yellow waters to the Kentucky shore that he knew like the back of his hand. Familiar landmarks cheered him. He shot a buffalo and cooked his first meal in four days. He was in sight of Boonesborough. He had kept his rendezvous with destiny.

It was a strange figure that came across the clearing into Boonesborough and said he was Daniel Boone. For weeks they had said Daniel Boone was a goner for sure this time. Even Rebecca's faith had failed and she had returned with the family to the settlements. Boone was sorry, yet glad, too, for she was safe. His brother Israel and Jemima, his beloved daughter who had married Dick Calloway, were there to give him a warm welcome. But it was no wonder Rebecca had gone. Many a husband and father had never come back across the clearing.

The news of the coming Indian raid roused the settlers to action. The neglected log walls were repaired and everything made ready for an attack, the swift short Indian attack with which the borderers were familiar. But weeks passed and no Indians were seen. Then another escaped white man brought in news that

Boone's flight had delayed the Indians. Boone then took a raiding expedition across the Ohio and burned an Indian village, getting back just a few hours ahead of the great war party of over four hundred Indians with some forty French Canadians under the direction of their officer De Quindre.

There were about fifty men and boys, besides the women and children, behind the log stockade when the Indians surrounded the clearing of Boonesborough. Instead of the usual sudden attack, an Indian came out of the woods with a white flag and by calling back and forth arranged for a parley. Every hour of delay meant a nearer hope of reinforcement coming in from Harrodsburg. Three of the defenders met Black Fish, Moluntha, and Catahecassa near the fort for a powwow. There was talk of friendship and peaceful surrender. The chief promised that the whites would be taken safely on horses to Detroit if they surrendered peaceably. There need be no bloodshed if the Americans would agree to abandon the fort.

Boone said he would explain to his people and in two days give an answer. He was glad to find that the Indians had heard from a white captive that there were several hundred defenders in the fort. The Indians believed their offer of safety was sure to be accepted.

Inside the fort the chances were talked over and argued and weighed after the democratic way of the backwoods. The odds were ten to one and worse against defense, and not a man, woman, or child would be spared if—But the tough cantankerous spirit of the frontier urged: "Go ahead or bust." They would not have been where they were if they had not been stubborn survivors of a rough, tough, restless race who lived and died in their own independent way by the rifle, the ax, the Bible, and the plow. So they sent back the eagle's answer: "No surrender," the answer of the sassy two-year-old baby democracy, the answer of Man the Unconquerable to the hosts of darkness—"No surrender."

The iron-faced chiefs and the ornery Frenchman De Quindre took the answer grimly back to their council, while the settlers got in their cows, corn, and water from the spring without interference from the Indians. The next move was an Indian trick which was perfectly transparent to Boone, but he took the chances of playing it to win time.

The Indians proposed a grand council of nine on each side to sign a treaty of peace, after which they would depart, they said, like lambs. The council sat under the sycamore trees within rifle shot of the fort. At a wave of the hat from the delegates the riflemen in the fort were to open fire and cover the nine men's dash back when trouble started.

All day they sat in the shade and smoked, talked, and ate while a fancy treaty of peace, including a sworn allegiance to the British Crown, was agreed on, to be signed tomorrow at the same place. In the night an ambush of Indians was set around the treaty tree. The next day when the nine appeared from the fort, Black Fish met them with eighteen powerful young braves. After the signing came the two-to-one hand-shaking. Two Indians grabbed for each white man and a mob jumped from the laurel to finish the job. Then the nine Kentucky wildcats let loose with teeth and claws, and the fur flew. Shooting began and the nine raced for the fort. They had won the first round.

Next day there was a great hubbub in the forest, bugles blowing and orders for retreat bawled out, and the pack horses were seen crossing the river at the ford. But the old border fox in the fort was not fooled. The gates of Boonesborough remained shut and the Indian trick failed. The real danger was an Indian rush on the gates under a heavy fire from all sides. This was what kept the riflemen waiting and watching at the portholes day and night.

But to charge across the clearing under the fire of Kentucky rifles was so contrary to the Indian way of fighting that all of DeQuindre's urging for a mass

attack was useless. Instead, the savages remained under cover of the woods, firing continuously. Day and night under the heavy encircling fire of the enemy, the riflemen stuck to their posts, blazing away whenever an inch of Indian hide was exposed to view. The women passed out the scant rations and scarce water, loaded guns when the firing was fast, molded bullets, comforted the children, and prayed the prayers of the pioneer faith. Each slow day under the burning sun was an eternity; each night they thanked the God of their Fathers that some protecting angel had kept the gates.

[6 1]

From high up in a distant tree a sniper began sending bullets inside the fort and Jemima Boone was hit. Boone drew a bead at two hundred yards on the sniper as he was reloading, and put a bullet through his head. The figure that pitched from the high tree was black Pompey. Colonel Calloway, of the old school, became irritated at Boone's cautious tactics and contrived an impressive wooden cannon. The roar and smoke of her first shot scared the Indians for about a mile out of range, but when the smoke cleared from her second blast she had burst wide open and was permanently disabled. But she was the wonder of the wilderness as long as she lasted.

More serious was the tunnel which the enemy was driving toward the fort.

It carried to the defenders the sinister fear of exploding mines that would breach the wooden walls. Day by day they could hear the digging come nearer. It wore on their strained nerves like the gnawing of a rat in the night.

Hour by hour a week dragged on. In the inky blackness of the seventh night a bright flame suddenly shot across the clearing in a long arc and dropped on a cabin roof. It was the dreadful flaming arrow. Now they were dropping fast on the pine roofs of the cabins. Worse yet, the savages had crept across the clearing in the darkness and started fagot fires against the log palisade on all sides. The spreading glow lit up the clearing as the hungry little flames ran along the shingles. Against the glow the frantic silhouettes of the defenders trying to beat out the flames drew stinging gun fire from the enemy. Suddenly a figure leaped up on a burning roof and in a fury of flame and bullets beat out the fire. When he had finished he calmly jumped down to safety. But the fires along the stockade were taking hold and the last remaining buckets full of precious water would be of no avail. The riflemen were standing at their posts holding their fire, waiting for the final mass attack, and women stood clutching their children. To Boone it seemed the last card had been played and lost. As the red light flickered over his set face, suddenly he felt a drop of water strike the back of his hand, and as he looked up heavy drops struck his face. In a few minutes the God-sent rain streamed down in drenching sheets. The burning stockade hissed, steamed, glowed, and went out. Something beyond human power had saved Boonesborough by the skin of its teeth.

Still the firing from the forest kept up incessantly. No one knew how near the tunnel was, but it seemed almost under their feet. The September pouring rain had soaked everyone to the bone. They would soon be passing around the last ration of food. Hope held desperately to ever slimmer chances. No Indian attack on a fort had ever been known to keep up so long.

Utter darkness of a night of lashing rain set in on the ninth day of the siege. In the fierce movement of the storm it seemed as though the savage demons of all the wild valley had come down for vengeance. It was a blind night when a man could not see the end of his rifle barrel. Nothing now could stop the mass rush of the savages across the clearing. The riflemen stood grimly at their posts in the pouring rain and waited. In the darkness time stopped. They shifted and growled, trying to keep their powder dry, and muttered to each other. At long last the night lifted. Out of the shapeless grayness the world was taking form. The morning came with no firing from the enemy, and the lookouts reported no signs of Indians in the forest. It looked like another false retreat. A scout or two came back with the news that the Indians were on the march this time for sure.

Then two white men crossed the clearing shouting and waving. One was Simon Kenton who had not been able to get through the lines. It was true that the Indians had gone. The white medicine was too strong. The spirits of the forest were beaten and the white gods prevailed. A surge of wild joy was in the hearts of Boonesborough when the log gates swung open and let out the starved cattle. There was whooping and firing to welcome eighty backwoodsmen from Harrodsburg, riding in too late for a rescue but in time for the celebration.

IV. KENTUCKY RISES

NOW THAT their scalps were saved and the surrounding forest peaceful again, the settlers went out and picked up the Indian bullets that lay thick around the walls. After the danger was over, the cowardly little meannesses of human nature came from their holes and bit venomously at the man who had saved their hides. Nothing less than a court-martial for Daniel Boone.

Already Kentucky had too many touchy colonels. Colonel Calloway was the ranking officer during the defense in which Boone had taken things into his own hands and won the day. It was Colonel Calloway who brought the charges and demanded that Boone be tried by court-martial. It was charged that he had acted for the British and had tried to betray Boonesborough into their hands. But the riflemen of the Wilderness Road knew their man too well for such nonsense. He was honorably acquitted and given the rank of Major of Militia.

As soon as his name was clear Boone started for the settlements to find Rebecca. Once more he was knocking on the cabin door to be welcomed in an ecstasy of joy by the loved ones who had believed him dead.

Many border families were eager to move into the new country, and Boone again found himself at the head of an expedition ready to ride through the Gap and over the rough Wilderness Road. Boone, remembering Colonel Calloway's cannon, lashed two small bronze cannon to the backs of strong horses to carry with them, the first ever brought into Kentucky.

With him was his brother Edward; and his old friend, Abraham Lincoln, would be joining the procession that slowly drifted through the Gap. The Lincolns had listened to Boone's stories. Now they had sold their Shenandoah farm and were taking the five children on horseback into Kentucky. Mother Lincoln carried in her arms the newest baby Tom. They were riding in the van of a procession of thousands of westward marchers that would be coming over the heartbreaking trail in summer and winter for years to come. Somewhere in the cavalcade would be riding nineteen-year-old Nancy Hanks with her baby Nancy in her arms. Little Tom Lincoln and baby Nancy riding through Cumberland Gap in their mothers' arms to grow up in Kentucky; Tom married Nancy and they called their first-born son Abraham after his grandfather, who had been killed by the Indians.

Great names and destinies for America were riding over the Wilderness Road into Kentucky in the 1780's. A settler's son, Chief Justice Robinson, in 1843, gives a close-up of the Kentucky pioneers: "Behold the men on foot with their trusty guns on their shoulders, driving stock and leading pack horses; and the women, some walking with pails on their heads, others riding with children in their laps and other children swung in baskets on horses fastened to the tails of others going before; see them camped at night expecting to be massacred by the

Indians, behold them in the month of December, in that ever memorable season of unprecedented cold, the hard winter, traveling two or three miles a day, frequently in danger of being frozen or killed by the falling of horses on the icy and almost impassable trace, and subsisting on stinted allowances of stale bread and meat. But now, lastly, look at them at the destined fort, perhaps on the eve of merry Christmas, when met by the hearty welcome of friends, who had come before, and cheered by fresh buffalo meat and parched corn they rejoice at their deliverance, and resolve to be contented with their lot."

When the Virginia legislature had called off Colonel Henderson's land deal, all who held claims under the Transylvania Company had to register and pay fees to the State of Virginia before they could own a foot of the Kentucky they had suffered so much to win. So to get legal title to their land, many of Boone's friends got together with their claims and the necessary fees to pay for them, and sent Daniel on the long ride to Richmond to put through the final deal that would at last make their homes and farms their own. Boone's great fame, his honesty and intelligence, and the fact that he had claims on pieces of land ranging in area from four hundred up to five thousand acres, made him just the right man for the job.

Boone rode off to Richmond happy in the high hope that all the tough days of hardship and poverty were over and that the lands and fortunes they had bought for so dear a price would now be lawfully theirs and their children's to have and to hold forever. In a few days he was back, crushed and disheartened. He had been robbed of every cent of the twenty thousand dollars, his own and his friends', money that represented all of their savings. The details of his misfortune are not known, but it was not strange that in those lawless times on backwoods trails a man traveling hundreds of miles alone with twenty thousand dollars in cash should be held up and robbed.

[70]

"Doubtless suspicion rested on him, not for dishonesty, but for carelessness; yet his friends, and those who suffered by his misfortune, retained entire confidence in his integrity, sympathized in his calamity, and cheerfully gave up their claims," wrote Colonel Hart in a letter dated August 3rd, 1780, after hearing of Boone's misfortune. "I have known Boone in times of old, when poverty and distress held him fast by the hand; and in these wretched circumstances I have ever found him of a noble and generous soul, despising everything mean; and therefore I will freely grant him a discharge for whatever sums of mine he might have been possessed of at that time."

Well they might. His whole life and the blood of his sons had been spent opening up a promised land of untold wealth—for others. He was entirely exonerated by many of those involved. The following June the legislature granted him a pre-emption of one thousand acres. But this, too, in time slipped out of his hands to claim jumpers in law courts.

There is a story that while he was in Virginia, Boone went to visit General Hamilton in the prison where he had been sent after his surrender to Clark at Kaskaskia. A strange meeting—the English general now a despised prisoner in a world turned upside down, and the Kentucky hunter who remembered the old kindness to him when a prisoner at Detroit and had come to do what he could to comfort his former captor.

And now Rebecca and Daniel and their family settled down in the newly-made county of Fayette, Kentucky; and when the settlers had to elect a representative to go down to the Virginia Assembly at Richmond and see to it that they got their share of the pie, whom should they elect but their most famous neighbor, the Honorable Colonel Boone? Daniel protested that he didn't have "book larnin' " and had never read the law. But it wasn't any use. Besides, Rebecca was proud of him, which didn't often happen. So he put on his Sunday

[71]

homespun suit that she had made. He listened patiently to her, which was unusual, when she told him to remember his manners and not to eat with his knife. He kissed his tall daughters good-by, mounted his handsome Kentucky mare, and rode down to Richmond feeling more embarrassed and uncomfortable than if he had been captured by Indians.

When he got there he found that Virginia was taking the long-drawn-out War of Independence very seriously. Since 1776 the war had been rolling south from Boston, and now Cornwallis had come to Virginia with a British army. In Richmond Daniel met young General Lafayette, who was supposed to keep General Cornwallis out of Virginia and wasn't quite making it. In fact, he and the army were leaving Richmond rather hastily and he had suggested that the Assembly do the same.

While the Assembly was meeting in little Charlottesville one bright day in early June, the British General Tarleton dashed into one end of town with his famous galloping Light Horse. But at the other end of town the august Virginia Assembly was leaving with even more dash and rapidity, so that the Tarleton Light Horse were able to round up only two or three of the legislators. It is an astounding fact that one of these was none other than Daniel Boone. The wily hero of desperate Indian escapes picked up and taken to Cornwallis by a couple of dumb British cavalrymen! It is hard to understand. Perhaps Rebecca's Sunday clothes fitted too tight for action, or Daniel's sense of his new dignities prevented his sudden departure into the forest. Like an Indian councilor he remained impassive and after a few days he was paroled as a noncombatant. During his parole he returned to Kentucky, later going up the Ohio into Pennsylvania to visit relatives and old boyhood scenes.

Boonesborough was filling up and spreading out. The log palisade was no longer the last barrier against the menace of the forests. But it was too crowded for the Boones. There was not enough elbow room. So they moved out about five miles and took up a farm that had belonged to his brother Israel. Here Daniel resumed his farming and hunting and Rebecca started another frontier home in the forest clearing. Although the Stations and outlying farms were growing in size and number, the vast new land was still an immense wilderness, filled with terror for the settlers. Out of it savage war parties descended on the

lonely cabins or lay in ambush along the forest trails and shot from cover at workers in the open clearings. Women fought as boldly as their men in desperate single-handed combat with ax and knife and rifle, as the fierce warriors forced into their burning cabins in the dead of night.

Indian expeditions equipped at the British base at Detroit crossed the Ohio to burn and plunder the Kentucky Stations. Counter-raids across the river by the enraged Kentuckians were as wild in savage fury. White man and red swayed in a deadly hand-to-hand battle of extermination across the Ohio valley. So close seemed the combat that either one might win. But the long-knives came on like the rising tide, as the forests fell and the red tribes perished amid the flames of their burning villages.

In the fall Daniel and his younger brother Edward had gone off together to the salt licks to boil down a supply for the winter's meat. While they were bending over the boiling kettles a sudden volley of Indian rifles broke out from the woods and Edward dropped dead. Daniel had just time to reach for his rifle and kill the savage that was reaching down for Edward's scalp. Before the others could jump from cover Daniel was gone. Once in the forest, he was able to hide his trail until an Indian dog took the scent and soon brought the redskins on his heels. Daniel waited behind a tree until the baying hound hove in sight and dropped him in his tracks with one of his famous long shots. He crossed a stream by a long swing on a grapevine and was gone over the hill.

Bryan's Station was a log palisade built on the same plan as Boonesborough but about twice the size, containing forty cabins. It was a border fort about five miles from Lexington. To the north lay the Ohio country from which the expeditions of plundering Indians and English swooped down without warning.

Scouts came in with the news of an Indian force on the way toward the

Station. It was a dark hour for the despairing Kentucky settlements. One of the Indians' leaders was a renegade white man named Girty. He was known throughout the Ohio valley for the fury and cruelty of his hatred of the whites. In every fort and cabin his name was loathed and despised. He hated and fought his own race with a cunning and brutality that surpassed the fiercest savage. But he was also known for one great deed of friendship and compassion. The Shawnees had brought into Girty's camp their white prisoner, Simon Kenton, who was so disfigured from running the gauntlet as to be unrecognizable. The Indians were determined to put him to the slow death by torture. But Kenton recognized Girty as his old comrade in arms at Fort Pitt. When he told Girty who he was, the renegade was deeply moved and put his arms around Kenton in a transport of affection and joy. Girty argued for his life with the blood-thirsty chiefs for hours, risking his prestige and authority in order to save his friend. In the end he succeeded and Kenton was spared.

But at the gates of Bryan's Station Girty was again the murderous beast seeking the scalps of the white men. That night one thousand Indian warriors silently invested the surrounding woods. In the fort were fifty riflemen besides the women and children. They were without a drop of water and all the cattle were outside the fort. They knew that if the men made a sortie to the spring they would be riddled from ambush. There still remained the chance that if in the morning the women and girls made their usual trip to the spring with buckets the Indians would not fire, in order not to spoil a surprise attack. So in the early summer morning the little procession of heroic women marched carelessly out of the gates across the clearing to the wood-spring. Slowly they filled their buckets within easy reach of the Indian tomahawks, and leisurely they trailed back into the fort and the heavy gates closed. Here is a processional for American memory.

[75]

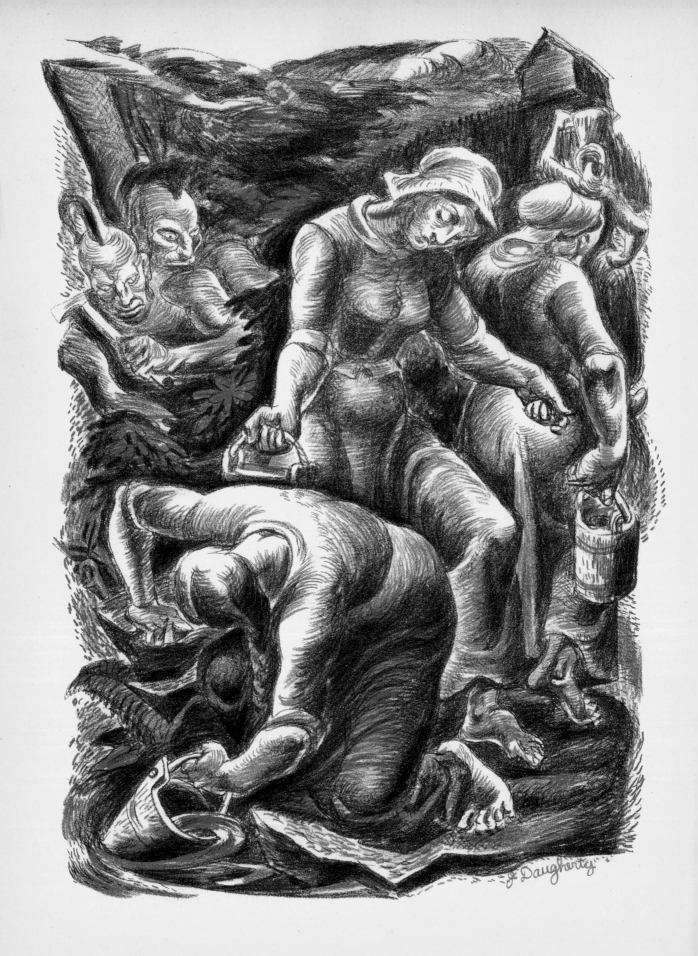

A small band of Indians appeared and pretended to retreat before a party of thirteen who made a sortie from the fort. The Indians were planning a mass attack from the other side of the fort, which they thought would be left undefended by the action on this side. They opened up with a full blast of everything they had, flaming arrows, warhoops, rifles, and quick rushes. These failed because of the deadly fire from the fort that never missed the mark.

In the meantime a rescue party of about fifty men from Lexington managed to get through the corn fields and underbrush into the stockade. By night it was so evident that the attack was a failure that the Indians gave up. Girty crawled under cover up within calling distance and tried to persuade the riflemen to surrender. He said re-enforcements and cannon were on the way. A sharp-spoken young rifleman named Reynolds gave Mr. Girty his views with such a hot handful of bad names that he permanently retired. During the night the whole expedition drifted off as suddenly and as silently as it had come. The Indian attacks were like tornadoes, brief and terrible.

The next morning the Kentucky boys for miles around were buzzing into Bryan's Station like mad hornets. Colonel Daniel Boone with his fine son Israel, and his brother Samuel rode in with a strong party of men from Boonesborough. By night there was a force of one hundred and eighty-two, with news that Colonel Logan with five hundred men was on the way. Nearly everyone was sure that by quick action they could overtake and destroy the fleeing Indians and take vengeance on the two white wolves of the border, Girty and McKee.

Boone had a look at the Indians' trail. It was suspiciously plain, the sure "come on" sign to an ambush. He shook his head. "Take it easy, go slow, wait for Logan," he advised. The old Indian fighter had trailed savages before most of these young hot-heads were born. Let some fool colonel call him a coward. The quiet hunter turned on his heel and walked off.

[7 7]

Next morning the whole pack were off on the trail. The Indians had followed a buffalo street as plain as day. They had left tree markings and abandoned equipment along the trail. To Boone every sign read: "Stop before it's too late." He was full of foreboding. He had seen the terrible shambles of a successful Indian ambuscade before. Besides, they were outnumbered five to one.

They followed on for about thirty-five miles and had now come out on the Licking River. They could see a party of the retreating Indians passing slowly along the buffalo trace and over the ridge on the other side as if inviting an attack. If the pursuers made a dash across the river they could easily overtake them. It was a moment for decision. A halt was called and the officers gathered around Boone. He pointed out that the Indians had passed over the barren ridge between two heavily-wooded ravines where the real force of the enemy probably lay in ambush. The best move was to wait for Logan with the re-enforcements and then out-maneuver the concealed enemy. At this point an angry, cocky major turned to the riflemen and called every man a coward who would not follow him. He dashed across the river with the stampeded Kentuckians whooping behind him.

As they advanced up the hill on the other side, Boone and the remaining men crossed the river to give what support they could in the foolish exhibition. They were now in the jaws of the trap and the Indians poured in from the ravines a murderous fire that crumpled and thrust back the reckless attack. The retreat turned into a panic as the whooping Indians broke from ambush tomahawking and scalping the white men running for the river. A dozen of the men on the best horses had forded the river and were headed for safety when one named Netherland, with the reputation for being a coward, stopped the horsemen and cried: "Fire on the Indians and protect the men in the river." Their brave stand enabled many to cross over unharmed. Young Reynolds racing for the river on his fast horse passed a staggering captain on foot. He jumped from the saddle, swung the exhausted man on the horse's back, and sent him galloping across the ford to safety. Reynolds managed to swim the stream but as he came out on the other side he was captured by a huge Indian with tomahawk and rifle. As he was led off through the woods the Indian stooped for a fraction of a minute to tie his moccasin. Reynolds snatched his rifle and sent his captor very suddenly to the Happy Hunting Grounds. Later he found his good horse and the grateful captain among the refugees at Bryan's Station. Through the drifting gun smoke sharp vignettes of desperate action stood out in vidid flashes and were gone. Boone had held the left wing to the last. His son was fatally wounded at his side. It was a terrible moment when he had to abandon the dead body and swim the river alone.

For the third time the ultimate tragedy of the wilderness had taken the thing nearest to his heart. As he dragged into Bryan's Station, he was thinking of Rebecca's face at the cabin door looking into the West.

He led Logan and the re-enforcements back to the battlefield but it needed no scout to find it. The black buzzards were sailing in slow circles overhead, and as the men forded the river the great birds rose heavily from their feast. The soldiers buried what the wolves had left but it was a ghastly task on that hot August afternoon.

Boone wrote a brief account of the Blue Licks battle to the governor of Virginia, Benjamin Harrison, not mentioning the loss of his son but making an earnest plea for troops. "The inhabitants of this country are very much alarmed at the thought of the Indians bringing another campaign into our country this fall. If this should be the case it will break up these settlements." He added: "But if they are placed under the direction of General Clark they will be of little or no service to our settlement."

[79]

The Kentuckians were resentful because they felt that Clark in the fort at the Falls of the Ohio could have prevented the Indian attacks. Now that the damage was done, Clark led a thousand mounted backwoodsmen up the Miami from Cincinnati burning out the forest villages. This dreadful punishment discouraged the Indians from making any large raid on Kentucky for many years, though the scalping parties continued to lurk in the forest and fall upon unprotected farms.

Daniel and his family were at Boone's Station when the courier galloped into Boonesborough with the great news that peace had been declared with England and that now they were the United States of America. Boone had been made the sheriff, the surveyor's deputy, and Lieutenant Colonel of Fayette County. He held these offices all at the same time.

He was busy surveying, hunting, and guiding settlers to new homes. Thousands of settlers in the years after the Revolution began coming by flatboat and forest trail into Kentucky. He was so busy helping them to fat farm lands that he neglected to protect his own claims by the necessary legal formalities. It was easy for claim jumpers to walk into court with the right kind of papers and oust Boone from his land. Finally he did not own a foot of the Kentucky he had helped to build. The still woods that he loved were falling under the axes. The fur-bearing citizens were vamoosing. The flower-strewn prairies were being laid out into neatly turned rows by bull-tongue plows.

But the name of Boone had become a legend echoing back over the mountains and across the sea. Mr. Filson, the school master, came down from Lexington to the Station especially to write his biography. What a story he must have heard! Mr. Filson embalmed it in elegant language and dullness and reflections on the beauties of nature. Boone was delighted with such an elegant book about his adventures and it became popular.

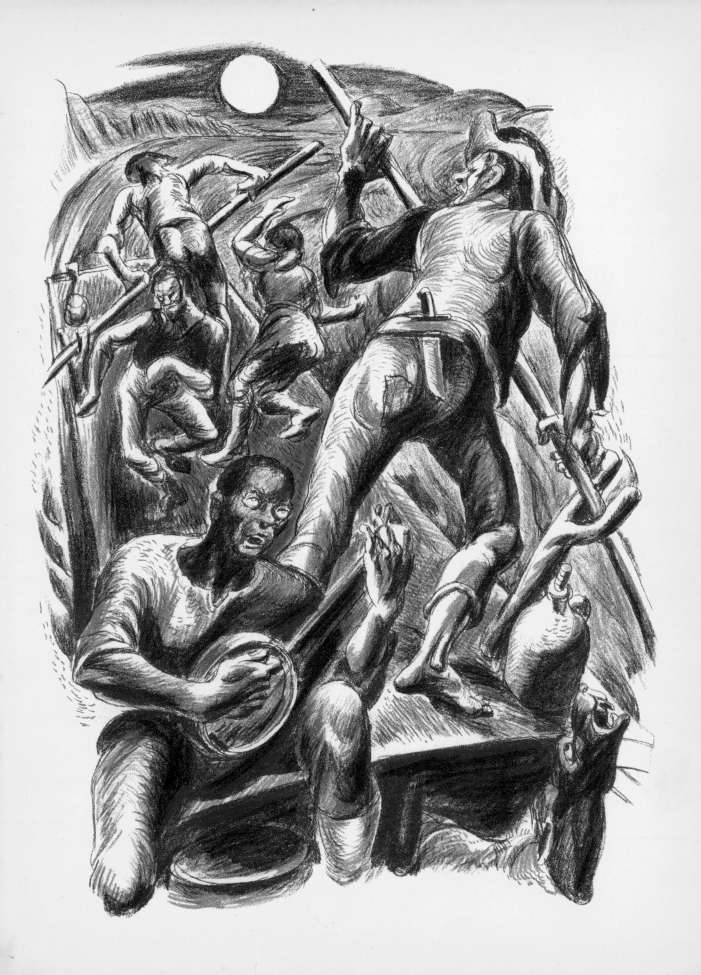

Settlers were now drifting down the Ohio in flatboats dodging Indian arrows and tomahawks. Those that got by landed at Maysville to go on into Kentucky. Boone often went there on business, and in 1782 the family left Boone's Station, moved down the river to Maysville, and ran a tavern and store for a while. Rebecca's cooking fed the hungry flatboatmen and greenhorns just off the river.

Trade was moving up and down the river and over the mountains—furs, tobacco, molasses, bacon, and ginseng, the curious root that went in Yankee clippers to China and made fortunes for New England. Daniel took a hand in all of this, dealing in horses and riding back and forth across the mountains with pack trains of goods. To be pushing on ahead of the restless stream of westward trekkers was good. But he was done with fighting. He had done his bit. He was through with Kentucky. It was a bitter memory. To think that he had not one foot of Kentucky land to give to his children! Fifteen years ago it had been all his for the taking.

He did not go west but east, up the river to Point Pleasant where the Kanawha flowed out of the Alleghenies into the Ohio and the ghost of Cornstalk on moonlight nights called to his braves: "Be strong, be strong." The Kanawha valley was still a backwoodsman's dream of heaven when the disinherited Kentuckian brought his sorrows and his fame to its hospitable cabins. Settlers who stopped off at Point Pleasant on a perilous voyage down the Ohio in 1789 went into the new store to do a little trading and swap river news and were waited on by a quiet woman called Mrs. Boone. They chatted with a pleasant man with deep-set blue eyes and high cheek bones. They were thrilled when someone said: "That's Daniel Boone." He had just been appointed Lieutenant Colonel.

The elections were everybody's business in a brand spanking new republic, so in 1791 when it was time for Kanawha to send a representative down to

the Virginia Assembly there was a big hurrah and shouting and speechifying for Colonel Boone. Wasn't he the only candidate that could write and could do surveying? So the Boones left the valley to go down to Richmond to the Assembly where Daniel had been twice before, the first time being the occasion of his remarkable capture by the British cavalrymen. The frontier colonel listened gravely to the elegant speechifying in the Virginia Assembly and voted for anything that benefited the folks back in Kanawha.

[8 3]

But before long Boone was moving up the Kanawha valley farther and farther away from the settlements on hunting trips and sometimes riding down to the river towns to trade furs. Occasionally he did surveying jobs for a grabbing land company or a lone settler.

To the new generations sweeping on he was like a page out of the past, a patriarchal figure around whom hung fantastic legends and romance. He was pointed out to strangers when he rode into the ragged streets of a sprawling boom-town. Being a curiosity annoyed him and he grew more and more uncomfortable in the raw new undergrowth of humanity sprouting up so rankly on the old hunting- and battlegrounds that were full of memories.

He was hearing stories about the rich hunting-grounds beyond the Mississippi—stories that reminded him of Finley, that stirred the same call to be moving on. It was like his lost youth calling again when young Daniel Morgan Boone came and told the old hunter that he was going with a party of settlers into the Spanish country, down the Ohio to St. Louis. The colonel was excited and pleased. Rebecca no longer protested. She had followed the many trails with a vast patience tempered by the long hard years.

Word at last came back from young Daniel that the Kentucky settlers had been granted fat farms on Femme Osage Creek about forty miles from St. Louis and that the hunting was fine. Rebecca saw it coming. She knew nothing could keep the older Daniel from going. He was full of the old enthusiasm, was happy again and busy in preparation. So the word got around that on such a day Colonel Boone was starting down to the river for the fabulous mysterious West. The Kanawha folk around Charleston gathered for a big farewell and barbecue and gave the Boones a whooping good-by as they rode down the valley. They loaded his best Kentucky horses and cows, his favorite hounds on the flatboats until it seemed very much like an amiable Noah's Ark. With some careful poling they

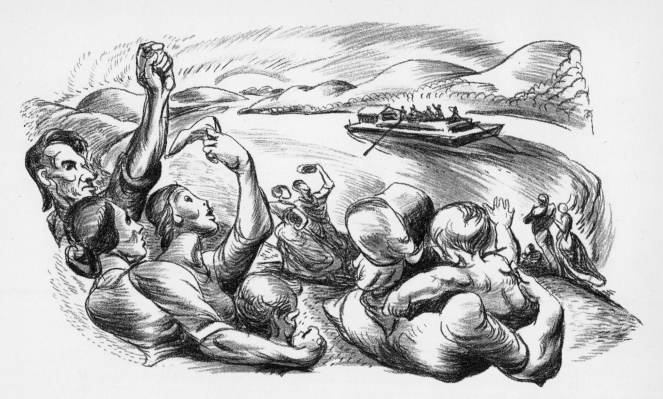

got out into the Ohio where the spring floods had speeded up the current and the long wooden sweeps held her in the channel.

No wonder Boone felt he was entering upon the happiest time of his life since his first trip into Kentucky. The voyage down the peaceful winding river was like a beautiful dream. When they pulled up at the little river towns everybody turned out to cheer and welcome them and beg them to stay longer. It filled the old man's heart with joy to feel that he was loved and honored by the people he had known so well. They drifted by the quiet shores he had known in times of danger, and past the mouths of rivers with silver-sounding names—Scioto, Miami, Wabash, Kaskaskia. On the left were the rivers of the promised land whose secret sources in the Cumberland Mountains he had sought out in the long ago, the Licking, Kentucky, Greene, Cumberland, Tennessee.

He was going west again, floating down the ample river in the beautiful Ohio spring, following the American dream.

[85]

V · LONG AFTERNOON

AT LAST the river voyage was ended and the Boones were crossing the Mississippi, the Father of Waters, into the little easy-going town of St. Louis. Boone was treading on the same spot where the great La Salle had built the first fort so long ago. He, too, had been a wilderness explorer of the farthest reaches, with his head full of great visions for a French empire of the Mississippi. And even before La Salle, at a point farther down the river, on a moonless night they had dropped into the dark waters the worn body of another seeker of far horizons, the Spaniard De Soto.

But on that July day in 1800 it was De Lassus, the Spanish Commandant of St. Louis, who welcomed Boone with a graciousness and respect that he had not known among the thankless Kentuckians. Here was an easy grace and gaiety of living that were foreign to the bleak Kentucky cabins. The French and Indians lived together on friendly terms and the Spanish and Americans were drawn together in their common antagonism to the British who had been a constant menace to the territory.

De Lassus knew a man when he saw one. He commissioned Boone as a government official or syndic. Besides the usual grant to a settler of one thousand arpents of land, he gave Boone a tract of ten thousand arpents with his office. The syndic was the government representative who administered law and justice in a lawless land. Boone administered primitive justice according to his own rules of common sense. He knew when a rogue deserved a lashing and he saw to it that he got it well laid on. There was no appeal from his decisions, so everybody had to be satisfied. The Femme Osage country was no place for claim jumpers under the Kentucky syndic. His duties as a judge were light in this simple and honest community. In the whole town there were only two locks, one for the government house and one for the calabozo.

So there was plenty of time for hunting and exploring trips up the Missouri to where the beaver and big game were plentiful. Jesse and Nathan Boone with their families had come to the Missouri country. Daniel Morgan, of course, was there and later came Flanders Calloway and his wife, Boone's beloved Jemima of the Boonesborough siege. They all lived within a half-day's journey of Daniel's cabin. Rebecca was happy amid friends, her children and grandchildren. It was almost another Boonesborough.

Mr. Peck, the traveling preacher, came to the Kentucky colony in Missouri and visited the old hunter. In his fine *Life of Daniel Boone* he describes him. "His high bold forehead was slightly bald and his silvered locks were combed smooth; his countenance was ruddy and fair, and exhibited the simplicity of a child. His voice was soft and melodious. A smile frequently played over his features in conversation. At repeated interviews, an irritable expression was never heard. His clothing was the coarse, plain manufacture of the family; but everything about him denoted that kind of comfort which was congenial to his habits and feelings, and evinced a happy old age."

He was the especial hero of a numerous race of grandchildren for whom he relived with zest his adventurous youth. They swarmed upon his knees and gazed wide-eyed into the fire as he told of the great siege of Boonesborough. These full years of overflowing happiness passed too quickly. History was moving on and dreamy Spanish St. Louis lay directly in her path. The nineteenth century was a husky pioneer baby that had climbed out of its cradle and was wading across the Mississippi. History was always catching up with the Boones.

In 1803 the tall red-headed Virginian, President Thomas Jefferson, bought the Territory of Louisiana for the United States from the little Corsican dictator who ruled Europe with artillery. The price was twelve million dollars; it was a big bargain for a westward-marching democracy.

In the crowd of cheering Americans who watched the stars and stripes raised at St. Louis were two young Americans, Captain Meriwether Lewis and his friend William Clark, younger brother of Clark of Vincennes. They had been personally appointed by the President to head an expedition into the West across the Rockies to the Pacific. On May 14th, 1804, "they proceeded under a gentle breaze up the Missouri," wrote Clark.

The old eagle stood looking into the West at the end of the trail as the young men started on a new enterprise that would blaze the path of empire to the Pacific. Boone had cut a path for history from the Yadkin to the Mississippi

[88]

and he was ready to roll back the years and ride off into the Far West. But Rebecca and his sons and grandchildren said no, and so he stayed in Missouri. He went on long trapping trips, alone or with a Negro or Indian for a companion.

Now his broad Spanish acres were slipping away. Again he had forgotten under the easy Spanish Commandant to sign the papers. The American commissioners were genuinely sorry but there was the law. The Louisiana Purchase that had doubled the area of the new republic and enriched it with untold wealth left Daniel and Rebecca landless and penniless.

But beaver skins were worth nine dollars apiece and Daniel was planning a big winter's work with the traps. He paddled alone up the Missouri River and made a snug camp well hidden in the bluffs. It was good beaver country and he cunningly set his traps. One morning when he was making the round of his traps he saw smoke rising near his camp. A little cautious scouting showed him the hunting camp of a large body of Indians. It was hostile country for white men; Daniel concealed his tracks as he made for camp and kept out of sight till nightfall when he could safely build a fire and cook food. Next morning there was a blessed blanket of new-laid snow which had covered his traps from the Indians. For a week he lay low and watched the Indian camp, praying that the prowling savages would not stumble on some sign of his presence. One never could tell how luck would break in the wilderness. He had enough dried meat to last a long time. It was twenty days before the snow melted and the Indians packed their camp on the poles of their travois and rode away. He told Mr. Peck he "never felt so much anxiety in his life for so long a period, lest they should discover his traps and search out his camp."

He came back in the spring to the Osage settlement with a big winter catch of fine beaver fur. Saying good-by to his family he packed up the bales on his horses and departed, saying only that he was going to Kentucky on business.

John James Audubon was a young Frenchman who had just come to Kentucky from Philadelphia with his lovely wife, Mary Bakewell, to make his fortune as a merchant. Instead, he was out in the woods studying and drawing birds. He was gaily letting the business go to the dogs. When Daniel Boone came back to Kentucky and sold his furs for a bag of silver dollars to pay his debts, John James Audubon was glad to meet him. They went squirrel barking together and sat up late at night while the old hunter told of Indian escapes and perils, and then lay down on the floor and went to sleep. Audubon thought he had met the rarest bird in all America.

They both had the curious mind to see and to know about America. They shared an enormous zest for living. They wanted to enjoy all of it first-hand, and were not satisfied to settle down and own a few thousand acres with a fence around it. They were a pair of shiftless traipsers, poor as Job's turkey most of the time, walking and riding and flatboating up and down the trails and rivers of America. The rougher and tougher it was the better they liked it. Audubon went everywhere from Labrador to Florida, from Boston to Missouri. He lived with Osage Indians and spoke their language. When he needed money he drew human birds for five dollars a portrait. He drew pen portraits, too, of the strange human birds he met everyhere. His keen eyes missed no detail of the roaring pageant of democracy marching westward.

Here is John James's own story of how he went squirrel barking with Daniel Boone: "Barking off Squirrels is delightful sport, and in my opinion requires a greater degree of accuracy than any other. I first witnessed this manner of procuring Squirrels whilst near the town of Frankfort. The performer was the celebrated Daniel Boone. We walked out together, and followed the rocky margins of the Kentucky River, until we reached a piece of flat land completely covered with black walnuts, oaks, and hickories. As the general mast was a good

[90]

one that year, Squirrels were seen gambolling on every tree around us. My companion, a stout, hale, and athletic man, dressed in a homespun hunting-shirt, bare-legged and moccasined, carried a long and heavy rifle, which as he was loading it he said had proved efficient in all his former undertakings and which he hoped would not fail on this occasion as he felt proud to show me his skill. The gun was wiped, the powder measured, the ball patched with six-hundred-thread linen, and the charge sent home with a hickory rod. We moved not a step from the place, for the Squirrels were so numerous that it was not necessary to go after them. Boone pointed to one of these animals which had observed us, and was crouched on a branch about fifty paces distant, and bade me mark well the spot where the ball should hit. He raised his piece gradually, until the bead (that being the name given by the Kentuckians for the sight) of the barrel was brought to a line with the spot which he intended to hit. The whip-like report resounded through the woods and along the hills, in repeated echoes. Judge of my surprise when I perceived that the ball had hit the piece of the bark immediately beneath the Squirrel, and shivered it into splinters, the concussion produced by which had killed the animal and sent it whirling through the air, as if it had been blown up by the explosion of a powder magazine. Boone kept up his firing and before many hours had elapsed we had procured as many Squirrels as we wished." It was fun for everybody but the squirrels.

A MID-OCTOBER afternoon. The oak and the maple were still in full leaf, but the oaks had turned to a crimson that burned in the mellow sunshine. Little yellow leaves were spiraling down from the maples that were blazing in a burnished splendor. Autumn was a parade of blood and gold, proud and splendid.

An old brown hound snuffed among the fallen leaves. The old hunter leaned lightly against a shell-bark hickory. His face under his broad hat-brim was a noble bronze mask fringed with silver hair. Under his arm he carried the long-barreled Kentucky rifle. He was tossing a silver half-dollar in his hand. Through his mind drifted the memories, gold and crimson. Long memories of Rebecca and Squire and Jamie Boone lingered and touched hands and drifted on. Kentucky was a pageant of leaf memories. The figures of Clark of Vincennes and Robertson of Watauga, Nolichucky Jack and Simon Kenton rode down the years, tough-fibered men of action who had been gallant companions. The solemn chieftains—his Shawnee father, Black Fish, and his friend, Logan, Cornstalk and Dragging Canoe, standing by the council fires—rose up out of the past. They had fought it out man to man. They had been great enemies and he, too, was a disinherited son of Kentucky.

He had sold the heavy bales of thick beaver skins for nine dollars apiece and with a fat bag of carefully-guarded silver dollars he had sought out old friends who had lent him money and forgotten, or merchants who had advanced him supplies for which he had never turned in barter or skins. Warm Kentucky hearts glowed to see the old man again. And he paid over the counter every dollar asked on past accounts. He said: "No one can say when I am gone that Boone was a dishonest man."

He was square with Kentucky, Kentucky for which he had given so much and taken so little, and he still had four bits. He felt rather rich. The rambunctious American eagle on the half-dollar gleamed in the late sunlight as he tossed it in the air.

He hummed the old tune that he used to sing in the Kentucky canebrakes.

He whistled to the brown hound and shouldered his long rifle. He would go back to Missouri now. His grandchildren would be waiting for him, waiting to swarm into his lap or to lie on their stomachs on the floor and gaze at the burning hickory logs as he told them the old stories. He would tell them about Black Fish, his Indian father, and how he lived when he was captured by the Shawnees and they made him into an Indian and washed his white blood away in the smoky huts of Chillicothe. They would laugh and say that he was still an Indian.

He had written a memorial to Congress telling them how it had been in the old days and what he had done for Kentucky. He explained how the Spanish Commandant De Lassus had said he wouldn't need the papers signed in New Orleans in order to hold his Spanish lands in Missouri. He should be allowed the lands by the American government. The memorial had got to Washington after a time and the committees had investigated and considered and recommended. So by an Act of Congress the government in Washington put it down on paper that the land which the Spanish government in Missouri had given him was really his after all. They said it was the right thing to do because "it was unjust as it was impolitic that useful enterprise and eminent services should go unrewarded." He didn't understand what that meant about its being "impolitic," but he remembered that his friend Mr. Henderson had been given four hundred thousand acres for his eminent services in getting Daniel Boone to build the Wilderness Road. So he figured that everybody was square.

It didn't much matter anyhow, now that Rebecca had gone on to the Promised Land. But that would be all right, too, for he would be going to get her soon. It would be just as when he had always come back from the wilderness and she would be waiting in the cabin door. They would be moving on together into the happy valleys.

He roused himself and went to the fire where he was roasting a venison steak on the ramrod of his gun. Some friends were coming and he rose to greet them. "Mr. Harding, the painter, has come all the way from St. Louis to take your likeness," they explained. He didn't quite know what it was all about. The

[94]

next day the young man came and asked him to sit very still while he painted his picture on oil-cloth. So he sat and talked of old memories and answered the young man's foolish questions. Had he ever been lost? He, Daniel Boone, lost! He thought back a while, shook his head, and said very slowly: "No, but I was right bewildered once for three days."

They were laying the corner-stone of a brand new state in St. Louis in September 1820. The Constitutional Convention was meeting in St. Louis to build a great new state for democracy right in the middle of the continent of America. When the news came that the mighty hunter had gone beyond the borders, beyond the ranges, the Constitutional Convention adjourned that day to remember

Boone—of Missouri, of Kentucky, of Carolina, of Virginia and Pennsylvania. Boone—Trail-breaker for destiny for a free people marching on.

So they took a day off for remembrance about humble, great-hearted men whose lives were a strong invisible substance for enduring corner-stones for these United States of America.

INDIANA STATE
T.C. LIBRARY

INDIANA STATE
T.C. LIBRARY